MW01046134

BIBLE
STORIES

Text by Ben Alex

Illustrations by
Gustavo Mazali

The Stanborough Press Ltd.

BIBLE STORIES
Stories of the Bible
First published by Scandinavia Publishing House
Copyright © 2004
This edition published by The Stanborough Press Ltd,
Alma Park, Grantham, NG31 9SL, England.
Copyright © 2006
Text by Ben Alex
Illustrations by Gustavo Mazali
Design by Ben Alex
ISBN 1-904685-21-8
Printed in China

CREATION

Genesis 1:1 – 2:3

The beginning

In the beginning there was nothing—
except for God.

God said, "Let there be light!"
—and suddenly there was light all
over.

Then God made the earth—the
beautiful earth where we live.

God fills the earth

The earth was full of water, but God made land in the water and filled the land with rocks and dirt, plants and trees, valleys and mountains, rivers and fields. The earth was very beautiful.

7

God makes stars and planets

God filled the sky with stars and
planets. He made the moon and the
sun to give us light and warmth.
Everything was in perfect balance.

God makes animals

Now God wanted to make animals - animals that swim, animals that run and jump. God even made animals that climb trees, and animals that fly high in the air! They all loved the earth, and God loved the animals He had made.

11

God makes people

Then God wanted to make friends. He created a man and a woman that looked like Himself. The man He called Adam, and the woman He called Eve. God enjoyed his friends very much.

14

The garden of Eden

God made a special garden for Adam and
Eve. He called the garden Eden. In Eden,
no one was upset, and no one was fearful.
Eden was a friendly place, and God was
very, very happy with what He had made.

15

Creation in the Bible

Then God said, „Let us make man in our image, in our likeness, and let them rule over the fish of the sea and the birds of the air, over the livestock, over all the earth, and over all the creatures that move along the ground."

So God created man in his own image, in the image of God he created him; male and female he created them.

God blessed them and said to them, „Be fruitful and increase in number; fill the earth and subdue it. Rule over the fish of the sea and the birds of the air and over every living creature that moves on the ground."

Then God said, „I give you every seed-bearing plant on the face of the whole earth and every tree that has fruit with seed in it. They will be yours for food. And to all the beasts of the earth and all the birds of the air and all the creatures that move on the ground—everything that has the breath of life in it—I give every green plant for food." And it was so.
Genesis 1:26-30

NOAH'S ARK

By faith Noah, when warned about things not yet seen, in holy fear built an ark to save his family. By his faith he condemned the world and became heir of the righteousness that comes by faith.

Hebrews 11:7

NOAH'S ARK

Genesis 5:1 - 9:29

Evil people

God looked at the earth and saw how evil people had become. He felt sad because He wanted people to be happy and loving towards each other. So God decided to start all over again— with a man called Noah.

21

God tells Noah to build a boat

Noah was a good man. He loved God and wanted to do what God told him. Now God told him to build a boat.

"But there's no water around!" said Noah.

"You wait and see," said God. "I have decided to destroy the earth in a heavy rainstorm. You will soon need a boat."

God also told Noah to bring animals into the boat.

"You and your family and all the animals will be safe in the boat," God promised.

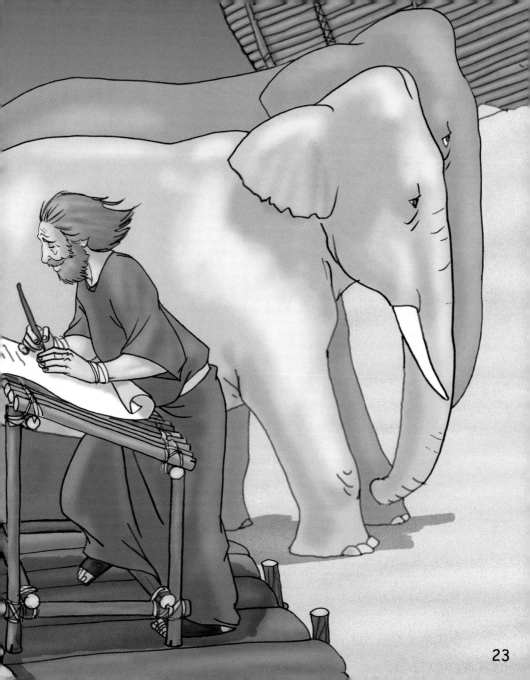

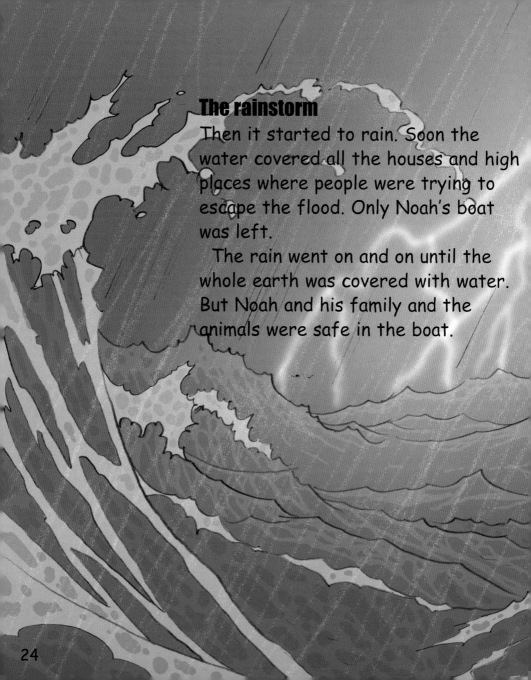

The rainstorm

Then it started to rain. Soon the water covered all the houses and high places where people were trying to escape the flood. Only Noah's boat was left.

The rain went on and on until the whole earth was covered with water. But Noah and his family and the animals were safe in the boat.

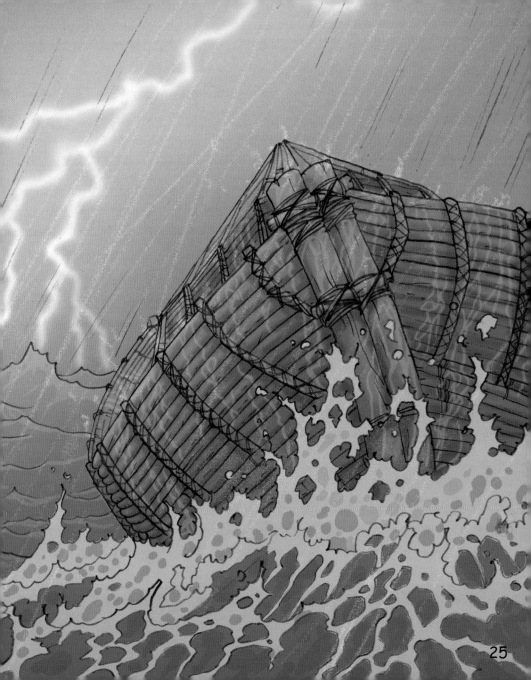

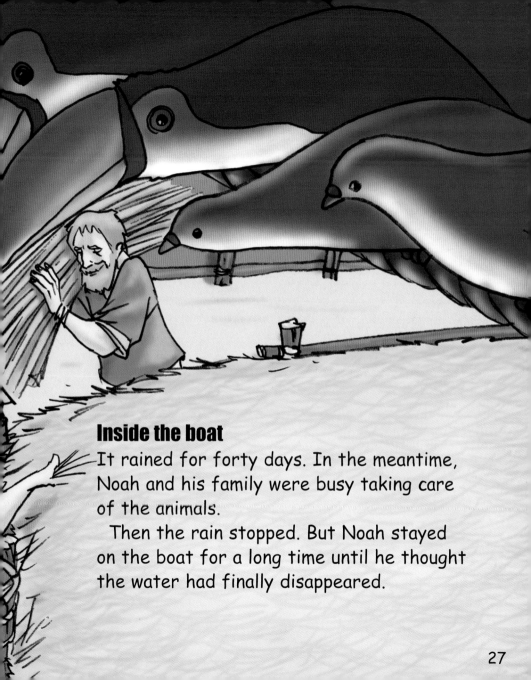

Inside the boat

It rained for forty days. In the meantime,
Noah and his family were busy taking care
of the animals.

Then the rain stopped. But Noah stayed
on the boat for a long time until he thought
the water had finally disappeared.

27

Noah sends out a dove

Before Noah let out the animals he wanted to be sure it was safe to get off the boat. So he sent out a dove. The dove came back with a green leaf. Now Noah knew there was dry land. It was safe for the animals to get off the boat.

29

God's rainbow

The animals spread out on the face of the earth, and Noah became the father of many people. God was happy and promised Noah never to destroy the earth again. As a sign of His promise He put a beautiful rainbow in the sky for everyone to see.

The rainbow reminds us that God loves us very much.

Noah's Ark in the Bible

The LORD then said to Noah, "Go into the ark, you and your whole family, because I have found you righteous in this generation. Take with you seven of every kind of clean animal, a male and its mate, and two of every kind of unclean animal, a male and its mate, and also seven of every kind of bird, male and female, to keep their various kinds alive throughout the earth. Seven days from now I will send rain on the earth for forty days and forty nights, and I will wipe from the face of the earth every living creature I have made."

And Noah did all that the LORD commanded him.
Noah was six hundred years old when the floodwaters came on the earth. And Noah and his sons and his wife and his sons' wives entered the ark to escape the waters of the flood. Pairs of clean and unclean animals, of birds and of all creatures that move along the ground, male and female, came to Noah and entered the ark, as God had commanded Noah. And after the seven days the floodwaters came on the earth.

Genesis 7:1-10

CHRISTMAS

CHRISTMAS

Luke 2:1—21

For to us a child is born, to us a son is given, and the government will be on his shoulders. And he will be called Wonderful Counselor, Mighty God, Everlasting Father, Prince of Peace.

Isaiah 9:6

A special baby

One day an angel came to Mary and told her she was going to have a baby. "This is a very special baby," the angel said. "His name shall be Jesus and he will be the Son of God!"

As soon as the angel had left, Mary ran home to Joseph, her husband-to-be, and told him what the angel had said.

No room at the inn

Mary and Joseph were on their way to Bethlehem, a city far away. Mary was pregnant and was soon to have her baby. But when they finally came to Bethlehem, there was no room for them at the inn.

Born in a barn

The inn keeper told Mary and Joseph they could stay in the barn for the night.

This very night Jesus was born. God's own Son was born among cows and sheep in a barn in Bethlehem!

Shepherds in the field

In a field nearby, some shepherds were taking care of their sheep. Suddenly they heard singing, and as they looked up, the sky was filled with angels! The angels told the shepherds the good news that the Son of God had been born in Bethlehem.

Three wise men

Far away in the East, some wise men heard of Jesus' birth. They thought that Jesus must be a king and set out to see him. They followed the bright star all the way to Bethlehem until they came to the house where Jesus was.

Gifts to Baby Jesus

The shepherds and the wise men were very happy.
They knew this baby was the Son of God.
The wise men brought gifts to Jesus to show how
grateful they were to God.

The first Christmas in the Bible

In those days Caesar Augustus issued a decree that a census should be taken of the entire Roman world. (This was the first census that took place while Quirinius was governor of Syria.) And everyone went to his own town to register.

So Joseph also went up from the town of Nazareth in Galilee to Judea, to Bethlehem the town of David, because he belonged to the house and line of David. He went there to register with Mary, who was pledged to be married to him and was expecting a child. While they were there, the time came for the baby to be born, and she gave birth to her firstborn, a son. She wrapped him in cloths and placed him in a manger, because there was no room for them in the inn.

Luke 2:1-7

EASTER

Christ has indeed been raised from the dead, the firstfruits of those who have fallen asleep. For since death came through a man, the resurrection comes also through a man. For as in Adam all die, so in Christ all will be made alive.

I Corinthians 15:20–22

EASTER

John 20:1—31

Jesus and his friends

Jesus was a good man who helped many people. He had many friends, and his closest friends believed he was God's own Son. But there were others who didn't like Jesus. They talked behind his back of how they could get rid of him.

Jesus is arrested

Jesus' enemies wanted to have Jesus arrested and put to death. So they decided to catch him at night while he was alone with his closest friends. The soldiers brought him to a judge and demanded he be crucified on a cross. Most of Jesus' friends were afraid and ran away.

Jesus on the cross

Only a few of Jesus' friends were with him when he was nailed to the cross. They were very sad because they had hoped he would live forever. But Jesus died on Good Friday and they buried him in a grave outside the city of Jerusalem.

Jesus' enemies were happy. They thought they had finally gotten rid of him. To make sure he wouldn't come back they placed a huge rock in front of the doorway.

The angel and the soldiers

Outside the grave sat two guards. Suddenly on Easter morning they heard a rumble and saw an angel roll the stone away from the grave. They had never seen an angel before, so they got very frightened and ran off.

The empty grave

Later that morning, Jesus' friends came out to the grave to mourn his death. But what had happened? The grave was open and there was no Jesus in the grave! Where could Jesus be?

Jesus' friends were scared. They didn't know who had taken Jesus' body away.

Jesus is alive

As they turned to go home, they suddenly saw Jesus standing right in front of them! Now they understood that no one had taken Jesus' body away. Jesus had simply risen from the dead! Jesus was alive!

Jesus' friends were very, very happy. They hurried back to the others to tell them that Jesus was alive.

The first Easter in the Bible

Then the disciples went back to their homes, but Mary stood out-side the tomb crying. As she wept, she bent over to look into the tomb and saw two angels in white, seated where Jesus' body had been, one at the head and the other at the foot.

They asked her, "Woman, why are you crying?" "They have taken my Lord away," she said, "and I don't know where they have put him."

At this, she turned around and saw Jesus standing there, but she did not realize that it was Jesus. "Woman," he said, "why are you crying? Who is it you are looking for?" Thinking he was the garden-er, she said, "Sir, if you have carried him away, tell me where you have put him, and I will get him." Jesus said to her, "Mary."

She turned toward him and cried out in Aramaic, "Rabboni!" (which means Teacher).

Jesus said, "Do not hold on to me, for I have not yet returned to the Father. Go instead to my brothers and tell them, 'I am return-ing to my Father and your Father, to my God and your God.'"

Mary Magdalene went to the disciples with the news: "I have seen the Lord!" And she told them that he had said these things to her.

John 20:10-18

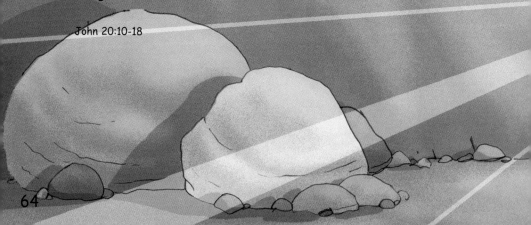